INTROVERT SALES SURVIVAL MANUAL

*How Quiet Salespeople Can
Thrive in a Loud Profession*

Red Stafstrom

ISBN-13: 979-8-88895-882-7
ISBN-10: 1477123456

Cover design by: Michael Stafstrom
Library of Congress Control Number: 2018675309
Printed in the United States of America

For Paddy Boy,
Miss you so much dude!
I wrote that book we talked about.

For Amys and Flynnie Fox
Love you all the love yous.
You are my favorites.

CONTENTS

THE GOAL

When I was researching this book, I looked into other Amazon reviews for introvert sales books. There was a common thread. No one wanted a sales book that loosely ties into introversion. They wanted a book where the two are married. They have their 2.5 kids and still hold hands while watching Jeopardy.

This is not a just a sales book. This is not just an introverts book. It is meant to be both.

Can extroverted salespeople learn something from this book? Sure!

Can introverts who don't work in sales learn something from the stories and anecdotes? Of course.

But this is really focused towards building a career where we can grow (and thrive) without suffering the burnout so many of us have dealt with.

Happy selling.

1. INTRO

"People always tell introverts to be more talkative and leave their comfort zones, but no one tells extroverts to shut up and make the zone more comfortable"

-UNKNOWN

There is no great way to tell you this. But odds are you are not going to change. It is not nurture. It is nature.

There was a study on temperment done by a Harvard Psychologist named Jerome Kagan. He divided the children into two groups.

One group was called inhibited or low

reactives. The are children who would not really react when there were loud noises or bright lights.

The other group was known as uninhibited or high reactives. These were the kids who would become cry the most when they were experiencing discomfort.

Kagan believed that a major difference between introversion and extroversion has to do with the way we see and respond to the world. That introversion and extroversion were tied to the way our brains deal with outside stimulus.

Kagan and his team marked these things down whether each child was high or low reactive and stayed in contact throughout childhood and into their teenage years.

This temperment, whether inhibited or uninhibited, became a great predictor of introversion and extroversion.

The high reactive children generally always grew up to become introverts like us.

By the end of the study, Kagan and his team believed you can predict introversion and extroversion accurately as early as four month old in most cases.

Now I understand what you are thinking. Wouldn't the loudest and most troublesome children grow up to be more extroverted?

Not at all.

Infants this age do not understand social cues. So their volume is tied directly to their level of discomfort. Introverts are more sensitive to stimulation so we would be the loudest toddlers when we were uncomfortable.

Think about how you know some people who get hungry, and others who get HANGRY. Same idea. The input of an empty stomach is the same for either person. But the HANGRY person feels it more acutely and it impacts the way they are as a whole.

But what does all this have to do with us?

I know, I just gave you a ton of words about stimulus, Harvard researchers, and other psych-speak that has nothing to do with revenue.... But it really does.

It has to do with who we are. It can predict how we learn and navigate our environments.

And most importantly, it can tell us how we can thrive!

Think about how your current sales team is managed. Are introverts and extroverts treated any differently?

Hell, are we even identified at all?

Maybe everyone took a Meyers Brigg test

when they were hired, but odds are good that data is sitting in a personel folder and has not been looked at since.

There is a major difference in the hardware that introverts and extroverts have, and yet most managers and organizations treat us all the same.

Introverts and extroverts are wired differently. To use a computer analogy, introverts tend to have stronger CPUs but less RAM. Extroverts have more RAM but less capable CPUs. This means extroverts are better at handling a lot of simple assignments, but introverts are better at focusing on a single complicated task.

That is really good for those of us on the quiet end of the spectrum! *Most sales these days are complex.* If the sale is simple, it would done with Facebook ads and landing pages. Any easy sale is turned into a funnel with chat-bots and automated drip campaigns.

Introverts like yourself are the future of sales. In the next 5-10 years AI will become more and more common, and simple sales will fall by the wayside. I expect we will see mass outsourcing of sales jobs to artificial intelligence. The same way so many manufacturing and call center jobs went to Asia in the late 1990's I expect to see an outsourcing toward artificial intelligence tools in the mid-to-late 2020's.

But what kind of salespeople will see their position's outsources to the digital wasteland? The kind of salespeople who read the sames script and make a few hundred calls per week.

That should not be you!

Experts like you who can skip the small talk and dive right into a the steps to solve a customer's problem will become a sought-after commodity in the business world.

It won't be easy, but this book is meant to

give you a path forward. It can help you to build your sales career to highlight all your strengths and minimize your weaknesses.

The **Introvert Sales Survival Manual** was written to help you understand what is special about you and use it to your advantage.

Introverts are not all clones of Ally Sheedy from The Breakfast Club. We are not all anime and video game nerds with no social skills.

We are simply people who need our alone time.

In the sales world, this is hard to come by. So let's structure our jobs to fit our comfort zone.

2. SET EXPECTATIONS

People cannot live up to expectations they do not know have been set for them.

- RORY VANDEN

I want to be totally upfront with you. I am going to ask you to do something in the conclusion of this book. It will cost you zero dollars, and can help improve both my life and hopefully improve the life another introverted salesperson like yourself.

I am going to ask you to cross a river of lava and get me the finest piece of black obsidian you can find. It should be no shorter than meter in length. Please cool it off before bringing it to me.

OK, I am just having fun. No need to cross a lava flow.

I just want a simple review.

Wherever you found this book (Likely Amazon) I am just asking you to fill out a simple review. Let me know what you did and did not like.

Not only will this help me, it will also help other introverted salespeople who may need a helping hand.

You do not need to do anything now, but if you make it to the end, please take the time to go back and fill out a review. I am sure you will be there at some point soon anyway.

3. WHO ARE WE?

*Introverts think before they act, digest information
thoroughly, stay on task longer, give up less easily,
and work more accurately.*

-SUSAN CAIN

Carl Jung coined the terms introverts
and extroverts.. However, he did so in
1910, at the infancy of psychology and
psychoanalysis. Jung studied directly with
Sigmund Freud. The relationship was so
close Freud considered Jung to be the "heir"
he was seeking to take the new science of
psychoanalysis forward.

When he described introverts and extroverts
he made it pretty simple. Introverts are
internally focused, extroverts are externally

focused. To really over-simplify, introverts spend more time in their own head. Extroverts tend to like to talk their ideas out.

There has been hundreds, if not thousands of books written about introversion, and I have gone through more than most. The period that stands out the most doesn't use the term "introversion" though. It uses a much more incendiary term.

Inferiority complex.

The Inferiority Complex was a term from Alfred Adler, another major name in early psychology. The term was meant to describe people with near crippling lack of self-esteem, but as the press got hold of it the term became much more wide-spread.

There are even points where it was abbreviated to simply "IC" in some articles. Articles about inferiority complexes still litter blogs for parents and teachers all the time. A simple google search found articles about inferiority complexes.

An article on Everyday Health says you can notice an inferiority complex in children if they:

- Generally avoid eye contact
- Are overly critical of themselves and others
- Refer to themselves as unlucky
- Frequently express embarrassment
- Repeatedly compare themselves to others
- Not trying new things because they do not think they will be good at them.

For most introverts, that list hits so close to home they are start thinking about installing cameras. In fact some of us may be accused by tavern-dwelling novice psychologists as having that very complex

This is what we are dealing with. Introvert means to focus inside, while extrovert means to focus outside. If anyone spends most of their time analyzing themselves, there are going to be times, possibly more often than not, when we come up short.

This does not mean we feel inferior. It can actually mean we have a more accurate grasp of our strengths and weaknesses than our talkative counterparts.

Most of us are simply more cognizant of who we are and how we operate best.

It is like playing a video game. We know which of our stats suck, and we even designed it this way. Those of us from the Tabletop Role Playing Game (TTRPG) world likely call this Min-Maxing. We know our strengths and weakness and put ourselves in the right situations.

Barbarians fail more intelligence checks.

Wizards fail more strength checks.

Doesn't make either one "weak". But either

can seem that way when put in the wrong situation.

I want you to take this mindest into this book. As an introvert, you likely have significant strengths, but also weaknesses.

Generally speaking, Introverts simply have more points in Intelligence and Wisdom.

Extroverts have more points in Charisma.

Both can be great at sales!!!

Even better, Charisma can be learned!

If you have Intelligence and Wisdom, I can help you learn the Charisma needed to succeed in a sales role.

This book is all about taking what you already have:

-        Personal insight

- A willingness to learn
- Authentic curiosity
- Love of information

And turn it into a path towards be one of the best salespeople you know.

Another major thing to consider is the way we recharge. I am going to go into this deeper in a later chapter, but for now just know that both introverts and extroverts have a battery that needs to recharge.

Introverts recharge their battery by being alone and focusing on intellectual activities. Our battery is drained by social activity.

Extrovert are the opposite. They recharge in groups and their battery ids depleted when they are alone. It is why so many extroverts struggled during the COVID shut downs in 2020.

Imagine having a very bad week, what are you going to do to unwind on Friday night?

Are you going to play video games or perhaps read a book? Or are you going to go out to the bar and hand out with a bunch of new people?

It is that battery that we need to focus on and protect.

4. MORE IS NOT BETTER

People who aren't used to quality chase quantity.

-UNKNOWN

How blunt do you want me to be?

I don't think most salespeople actually do sales. They try, but that is not how their job is actually structured.

Most of us work in what I have been calling Key Performance Indicator (KPI) Factories. By this I mean we are given a desk, a phone, and a computer along side a KPI requirement that we need to have every day/week.

Make 50 phone calls a day.

Send 30 emails.

Create 1 post.

Et cetera, et cetera, et cetera.

You see this is not sales. This is little more than a mass production of feel-good statistics for micromanagers.

Sure, I can conceed that these activities, when done right, lead to sales. But that is not a strategy that works long term.

Unless you are working in an industry where you have infinite customers, there will always be a significant downside to high volume strategies. People are way more likely to write a negative review thann they are to write a positive one. And simply playing the "numbers game" will lead to trashing your business' reputation. It will also lead to burnout and high employee turnover.

(FYI, If you work in a place like this, saying this out loud will probably not get you employee-of-the-month anytime soon.)

Most sales managers see the world like this.

1,000 calls = 10 appointments = 3 sales.

Knowing this, let's say you work at a company that just got Series B funding and that manager is now on the hook for 2x as many sales. What is their solution?

2,000 calls rather than 1,000.

Boom, double revenue. Right?

What if they need to triple revenue?

3,000 call.

And while this may works from an organizational standpoint, it does not work for YOU!

What if you, personally, want to double your sales? Can you honestly double the amount of outbound you are doing right now AND keep the quality at the same level?

OF COURSE NOT!!!

Going from working 40 hours to 80 hours is not the answer. That is how you deplete your battery and burn out.

Something has to break. So those of us on the introvert side cannot just resort to the same math question our extroverted co-workers can.

So what can you do? You can focus on efficiency.

You can move away from the numbers game and play a game you can actually win!

5. BETTER IS BETTER

Focus on being productive instead of busy.

-TIM FERISS

This is our path.

If we cannot spray-and-pray our growth strategy, we need to change the later part of the equation.

The answer is not more calls, we need to get more efficient.

We need to move from

1,000 calls = 10 appointments = 3 sales

to

1,000 calls = 20 appointments = 6 sales.

I made it seem really simple. But in reality it is one of the hardest things you will have to do. Doubling output is a lot simpler than doubling efficiency. It is not just about increased effort and clocking more time on the phones. It requires complex problem solving, strategizing, and research.

Good news! These are things introverts tend to be really good at!!!

Now let me give a simple disclaimer. Some organizations do not want you to go off book. They gave you a script, word tracks, and everything else. experimentation is discouraged if not outright forbidden. DO NOT GO EXPLICITLY AGAINST YOUR BOSS' ORDERS WITHOUT PERMISSION.

The good news is our path is clear. We have a

good goal in mind. It likely looks something like this. (Adjust it for your numbers)

I will go from a 1% appointment rate to a 2% appointment rate by {DATE}.

It does not have to be as simple as this but take 10 minutes and come up with the right goal for you. Focusing on efficiency is the key. More sales in fewer conversations is the goal. It is how we protect our social battery.

I want you to write this goal down in a clear way. Here is the format I always suggest.

Go from (*Current number*) to (*Goal number*) by (*Date*).

There are plenty of other books out there that talk about goal setting, but this is a solid start. You do not need anything more complicated than this.

Next, create a scoreboard. Put it somewhere you see all the time. DO NOT NEGLECT THIS STEP!!!! It can be as little as a post-it you update once a week. For the rest of this book, we will focus on appointment set rate, but it could be close rate or average deal size. Almost anything. The goal is for you to make the same commission in half the conversations.

A good scoreboard will look like this. You will be tempted to overcomplicate it. DON'T.

Go from 1% appointment rate to a 2%
appointment rate by end of quarter

Week 1 : 1.09%

Week 2: 1.14%

Week 3: 1.12%

Week 4: 1.20%

Week 5: _____

Week 6: _____

Take the time now to write out your goal and design your scoreboard. Focus it on efficiency, not revenue. By doing this, you can now have clarity on what you want to accomplish as you continue through the book.

6. BE LAZY

Efficiency is intelligent laziness.

-DAVID DUNHAM

There are a lot of sales pros talking about the right mindset for sales. You hop on LinkedIn for any amount of times and see what I have been calling Glitter Speak.

Hustle Harder.

Outwork Everyone.

Sacrifice today so you don't have to tomorrow.

No one ever grows in their comfort zone.

Bull.

Fucking.

Shit.

Do you think locking your favorite office plant in a closet will make them thrive?

Have you ever gone to one of those mall pet-stores and seen all the dogs in the kennels for 24 hours a day? Are they living their best life?

NOT AT ALL!

So why would you think it works for human beings?

This is about survival, and you are not going to be the one person in the world who only needs 500 calories and 3 hours a day of sleep to live long term.

Get rid of hustle.

BE LAZY.

Start with a simple premise. Assume your work day gets cut from 8 hours per day to 4 hours per day, but you need to create the same results. What are you going to do?

We increase the things that work best.

In the last chapter you should have written an efficiency goal. In the example I used, I tried to double the efficiency rate. I set a goal to go from 1% appoint setting up to 2%.

But what if we did not have the time to make 1,000 calls to set 20 appointments?

What if we could only pick up the phone 20 times and you need to schedule 20 appointments?

That is a fun question, isn't it? How do we go from 1% to 100% success rate when we pick up the phone?

What if there is a way you can cut your "work" by 99% and make the same income?

Let me be clear, there probably isn't, but for the moment let's play in the world where it is. What is your first step? How do you uncover this magic?

What do these 20 people have in common? Where do they hang out? What issues are they having? Where are they already looking for answers? And most importantly, how do we get there before they even know they have a problem and get a dozen other vendors involved?

Now is there any way to identify these people BEFORE dialing a single person or sending a single email?

What if you look back on these twenty appointments and realize six came from referrals from past customers? Is there a way to talk to past customers and get more referrals? Maybe you can write one email to a current customer asking for referrals and possibly get 3 or 4 appointments. Boom! With one email you went from 10 appointments to 13 or 14.

Now think about what the calls that do not book appointments have in common. My guess is 75 percent were voicemails. Voicemails have a less than 5% success rate. What if you sent a text when someone didn't answer instead? If you are like me, you probably like texting more anyway.

There are lots of different ways to get more appointments WITHOUT EVEN PICKING UP THE PHONE!!!

This is how we start preserving your social battery! It is by learning how to get sales without using any energy on small talk or repeated voicemails.

7. THEY DO NOT NEED TO LIKE YOU.

I'm famous today. People like me today. Might not like me tomorrow. You can't count on it.

-DAVE CHAPELLE

Ok, yes there are lots of ways to get more efficient before the call, but what about when you are on the call? How do you increase the likelihood of getting the appointment?

First, let's think back to who we are as introverts. What are our strengths? We like deep critical conversations over small talk. So why are you still pushing the same old "the weather is crazy around here" or "traffic is so bad". Salespeople have been so conditioned toward relationship building we miss what is right in front of us.

Simply put, *they do not need to like you.*

I know, that sounds like blasphemy. But hear me out. Keenan explains this really well in GAP Selling.

Let's look at this simple four-square.

	Incompetent	Competent
Great Relation ship (Liked)		
Bad Relation ship (Dislike)		

Let's knock the obvious ones out of the way first. No one wants to work the incompetent person they dislike, and everyone wants to work with the competent person they like. So let's mark that down.

	Incompetent	Competent
Great Relation ship (Liked)		☺
Bad Relation ship (Dislike)	🚫	

Easy enough, right?

But what happened in the other two squares? Let's say there is someone I really like but they are not good at what they do.

I love my wife. She is my favorite person in the world. I am not letting her do surgery on me.

What about all your friends and family members who just got their Real Estate license or started selling some multi-level marketing trash?

You love them, but you are not going to work with them anytime soon.

Likewise, let's look on the otherside. These are the people you do not like but are extremely competent. Do you know who likely falls in that category?

Amazon.

Wal-Mart

Verizon.

Comcast.

Wells Fargo.

Simply go to Google and type in "Least popular companies in the world". Odds are you will find a list of 50 multi-billion dollar businesses that are hated by a large chunk of the population.

Yet they still make sales.

Millions of them.

So what does our chart look like now?

	Incompetent	Competent
Great Relation ship (Liked)	⊘	☺
Bad Relation ship (Dislike)	⊘	☺

The fact is we buy from people we do not like ALL THE TIME. So, when people tell you it is most important that people like you, it simply is not true. It does not even match your own personal experiences. Yet we keep saying it.

Yes, it is great to have people like you, but it is not the difference maker. Being seen as smart and capable is.

Do you want more proof?

Easy!

One of my favorite sales books is *The Challenger Sale* by Matt Dixon and Brent Adamson. Through their considerable research, they found that salespeople tend to have one of five personalities.

- **Hard Worker**
- **Relationship Builder**

- **Lone Wolf**
- **Reactive Problem Solver**
- **Challenger**

Now given the title of the book, it is safe to guess that the last profile, the Challenger, works the best. And you would be right. Challenger style salespeople make up 40% of all top performers in the B2B sales space.

Relationship builders accounted for only 7% of top performers. Even though so many companies chase relationship style salespeople, they are the least likely to become top performers.

Dixon and Adamson go into more detail as to why in their book, but the simple answer is buyers do not need a friend.

They need *trust.*

No, those are not the same.

If you are a Batman fan, you probably know this line from Batman describing Ra's Al Ghul. "Ra's Al Ghul is many things, but a liar is not one." Batman may not always trust Ra's Al Ghul's motives, but he does trust his honesty and credibility.

Let me tell you a story. Before my wedding I went to a Men's Warehouse and a more boutique store to find the suit.

I went to Men's Warehouse first, and found a suit I really liked. It was a dark blue that bordered on black. I liked it, but didn't pull the trigger.

I then went to a smaller place where there was an older man with a thick Greek accent. I found another suit, and it was a similar color.

The older man winced when I went to try on the jacket.

Yes, winced.

You see, I have red hair and pale skin. And in the dark colored suit, the older man said I looked like I worked at a funeral home.

He told me that in that suit I would look like a member of the Addams family.

Snap-Snap.

I ended up with a brighter blue suit, and I am so much happier. And my wife didn't run screaming from the alter.

I say this because someone who is too relationship focused may shy away from the truth. Sellers do not need to hear their opinions simply parroted back to them.

Simply put, buyers want someone who are OK being awkward.

If you are reading this, odds are you have felt uncomfortable a number of times in a wide array of social situations. THIS IS

YOUR SUPERPOWER! You can use those experiences to thrive in the sales world.

All of this should be a sigh of relief. You don't need to make asinine small talk. You don't need to become best friends, have sleepovers, and do karate in the garage. You just need to prove you know what you are talking about.

You need to be the expert that will help them get to where they are trying to go.

You do not need your customers to like you. Yes, it would great, but that is not the make-or-break part of a sale. that many other sales books make it out to be. Being the best market option is more important than being liked in the world of capitalism.

But what happens if you are not the best company. Not everyone is a market leader. Well, now is when you show you can provide something the other guys can't. You can provide expertise, consulting, and a massive network of people in similar situations.

Think about the position your customer is in. If you are in the B2B space, can you picture them walking into their board of directors and saying "I went with this software because I really like Ryan."

OF COURSE NOT.

But, if Ryan brings a wealth of industry knowledge and a network of contacts in the industry that is a very different matter.

They don't work with you because they like you. They work with you because you are damn good at what you do.

8. YOU ARE THE EXPERT

Trust = Character + Competency

-STEPHEN M. COVEY

So if your customers do not need to like you, what is it that they need to move forward?

Trust.

It is that simple.

I know, that sounds very similar to relationship building, but it isn't. I can trust people to do a task and not like them.

Have you ever had a doctor you did not really like? Maybe they were in a hospital setting and had a miserable bedside manner. Even though you did not like them, I am willing to bet you still followed the treatment plan they gave you. Have you ever listened to a plumber or electrician that you did not particularly like? I am sure you have. And I have too.

The reason we listen to people we do not like is because they are competent in what they do. They have a level of expertise that we do not.

So why not do something to make yourself the expert?

I am not saying you need to get your doctorate or electrical license. But you can do something else to show off that you are an expert in your field.

I wrote the first draft of this book in a single day of deep-focused time. It took me less than a week to upload it to Amazon and create a product that I can sell or send to people in my field who are looking for services like mine.

Odds are you can produce something very similar in your field. One Saturday of work can help you drastically increase how competent people think you are.

In his book **The Speed of Trust**, Stephen M. Covey wrote that *Trust=Character +Competence*. By creating a medium-content book and sending it to your potential customers you can greatly increase the level of perceived competence.

Also, how many other salespeople do you know that wrote a book? How much more do you stand out from your competitors by having a simple e-book available from Kindle Direct Pubishing?

Now, rather than having conversations, you can simply have your E-Book on Amazon. You can send it to your prospects by email.

Just take one problem your customers have that you help solve and write a short e-book.

I am also a fan of jumping on other people's podcasts or recording Youtube videos. I know to introverts this idea can be paralyzing. There is no getting around that other than realizing one hour of discomfort can save you from dozens of hours of discomfort if you create the right kind of content.

Being a guest on someone's podcast is simpler than ever these days. There are Facebook groups devoted to simply finding or being a guest. One post can help you book an show. Now, in one conversation, you are able to talk to their entire audience rather than having dozens of conversations one at a time. You can also use clips from that podcast in your marketing and emails.

You can do the same thing with videos on YouTube. Simply go down your company's Frequently Asked Questions list and record a short videos on each. Boom! You now have a bunch of micro-content to upload to YouTube and send in emails!

I get that this is terrifying, but is it really any more terrifying that then the cold calls you do?

Even if it is, is it more uncomfortable than 10?

20?

100?

These are things you do once and can re-use over and over again.

The goal is to have more results in fewer conversations. That is what it is all about!

9. YOUR NEW INVISIBLE BEST FRIEND

Everyone is not your customer.

-SETH GODIN

Remember when you were a kid and you had an invisible best friend? We are going to go back to that.

No I am not crazy...... OK maybe I am crazy. But trust me on this one.

The first step to getting the efficiency we are looking for is making just such an invisible best friend. But given this is sales, we are going to use a fancy acronym for it.

Our invisible best friend will be called our Ideal Customer Profile (ICP).

If you have been in sales a while, you have probably heard this term thrown around, but you never thought of it as a person. It was probably more of a bulleted list. For example it usually looks something like this.

The people we help are:

- *SMBs with 10-30 employees*
- *Saas Sector*
- *Some level of Venture Capital backing (Series A/B/C)*
- *Typically use Salesforce or Hubspot*

This is a good start, but we want to understand the PERSON.

In Russell Brunson's book ***Expert Secrets***, he tells a story about a man who is trying to sell beauty products to Sally Beauty. As he is selling, the people in the meeting say "You know, I do not think Kristen will like this."

The sales guy didn't understand. He replied "Of course she will. Can you call her in here. I am sure she will love it."

They couldn't. Kristen was not real.

Kristen was their ICP. Whenever they looked into a new process or product, they thought about 'Kristen'. This was the person they use to write all their marketing materials and who they kept in mind when they write any content.

On that note, Hello Ryan!

Ryan is my ideal reader profile for this book. He is the person I have in my head as I have been writing this book.

Here is what I wrote about Ryan. Let's see how close I got.

- 28 year old male
- 4-year degree in Business
- Has worked multiple sales companies
- Currently an SDR in a SaaS company.
- Not married, but has a significant other
- Stylish, but not in a suit-and-tie way. Think sneakerhead
- Likes / wants to travel, but mostly to modern nations.
- Plays video games in his spare time.
- Smaller family, but not an only child.
- Always has headphones nearby.
- Has a favorite place for Pho.
- Night owl, not an early riser but still trying.
- Does not like Facebook, but can get lost on Instagram or TikTok.
- Just starting his personal development journey.
- In the top third of salespeople, but not at the very top.

My guess is that if you are reading this book, a fair number of these hit home for you.

Can you say you know your ideal customer this well?

You should.

Take a few minutes now and imagine your ideal client. This can be modeled off of a customer you already work with that you really get along with well. Give them a name and write out a list like the one I just did.

Take it a step farther and get some stock photos. Put some of them on your desk to help you know who you are speaking to when you are writing content.

I understand it seems crazy now, but look through your own text messages. I bet you write in very different styles depending on who you are talking to. I write very differently when I am texting my wife, dad, brother, or college buddies. And ICP helps you write in a way that will get a response.

I received this message on LinkedIn today.

How are you doing today with your wonderful families and friends,how is the weather condition over there??

You are about halfway through this book. Do you think this resonated with me?

Do you think I even responded?

This is why having a clear ICP is so important. without it you do not even get the opportunity to sell anything at all.

10. WHERE TO TALK

Whatever pain you cannot get rid of, make it your creative offering.

-SUSAN CAIN

When I consult with companies about their marketing strategy, I see a lot of them spending money on bad marketing. These are things they dump a lot of cash into which they do not get a Return on Investment (ROI) from.

Let me ask a serious question.

When was the last time you called the phone

number on the bottom of a billboard?

What about the last time you got some kind of laminated postcard in the mail for windows or siding? Have you ever called one of those?

Can you recall the advertisement that was on the shopping cart the last time you went to the grocery store?

I cannot tell you how many companies still use these methods for marketing. It leads me to ask one simple question.

Why are you behaving differently as marketers than they do as consumers?

I make very few friends asking this question. Billboards, shopping cart ads, and mailers can costs thousands of dollars every month, and these people are just setting it on fire in some cases. They do not even have a good way to track the return.

Now I am going to ask a question that may make you hate me just as much.

> *When was the last time you
> answered a cold call and bought
> what they were selling?*

If you built you career around cold calling, that question can really hurt. But it is the epitome of expecting your customer behave in a counter-intuitive manner. You are asking them to do something you likely never will.

So how do we fix it?

That is simple. We stop cold calling. We do our research. We ask questions. We build a pile of kindling in order to warm the call up BEFORE we pick up the phone.

This is done through a combination or research and referral. It is about creating the strategy where you do more than plug numbers into a phone system and read a script. You have to be better than that.

You want to create an environment where they want to talk to you BEFORE They talk to you. Writing a book, having a YouTube Channel, or creating social media content relevant to your ideal customer is a great start.

I also suggest commenting on their social media content or speaking to someone else in their organization. I will explain how to do this more a bit later.

Overall, the biggest problem with cold calling is the COLD part. Stop making cold calls and start pre-heating the conversation. In the next chapter I will explain what and how you should research before making contact with a prospect.

11. YOUR CUSTOMER'S MIND

Before you criticize a man, walk a mile in his shoes. That way when you do criticize him you will be a mile away and have his shoes.

-STEVE MARTIN

We have talked a lot about behaving the same way as a marketer/salesperson as you would want to have as a customer. Now I want to take it a step further. I want to put you in the mind of your typical customer.

Who do you think of when you think of a salesperson?

Seriously, where does your mind go? Who do you picture as the prototypical salesperson?

I want you to imagine that person. Are they male or female? What does their hair look like? What clothes are they wearing?

I am going to take a wild guess. You probably thought of an attractive white man with brown hair and business casual attire. Am I right?

Or you may have thought of a mentor who taught you the ropes.

Who do you think our customers think of?

Well, think about the most famous salespeople in movies.

Gordon Gecko from *Wall Street*.

Seth Davis from *Boiler Room*.

John Candy from *Planes, Trains, and Automobiles*.

Danny Devito in *Matilda*.

Alec Baldwin in *Glengarry Glenross*.

Robin Williams in *Cadillac Man*.

While these actors did an amazing job, and some of them have their moments, do any of them make you feel all warm and fuzzy about sales as a profession?

In fact do any of these characters really seem trustworthy?

That is what you are up against.

That is the image that crosses your customer's mind when they get cold call.

I do not say this to make you nervous.

I want you to understand the discomfort your customer feels because the stereotypes against our profession are significant.

Here is the good news. You do not have to do much to exceed expectations.

The bad news is you cannot behave like a "salesperson."

No customer, ever, said "you know what? I wish this experience was more sales-y". But there is a soldi chance a manager may have said something similar.

So how do you stop behaving like the worst stereotype of a salesperson? *You do it by giving away good information.*

At this point, you should have a really good picture of your ideal client. If not go back to the Invisible Best Friend chapter. How much money do they make in a year? How much does that equate to an hourly rate? How can you offer a return on their TIME investments that is significantly higher than their hourly rate?

If you want to know your ICP's hourly rate, you simply divide their income by 2,000. (50 weeks x 5 days x 8 hours). This means someone who makes $200.

So if your ICP makes $500,000 per year, they have an effective hourly rate of $250. *Asking them for an hour-long meaning is like asking them to hand you a $250 to listen to you speak!*

What do you offer in return?

This is the price of a good concert ticket. What are you offering in return to make them say "Wow, I would be happy to pay that again!"

To paraphrase Neil Rackham, you want to create a sales experience so good people would be happy to pay you for it.

You need to create the right mindset going

into the meeting. I know if my ICP makes $500,000 per year, their time is worth $250 per hour. I want to make sure that in that meeting, I can help them learn something about their business that can create a 10x return on that investment. So if I am asking for an hour of time from someone who makes $500,000 per year, *I am actually aiming to offer insight and advice worth $2,500 minimum.*

Sidenote: Let me also say, the phrase "add value" is overused. When I hear those words, I imagine one of the old drawstring style dolls similar to Woody from *Toy Story* dressed as a business man. It would repeat phrases like "add value" or "we need to pivot" over-and over again. The worst point, you can pull that string during any meeting you fall asleep in and still sound like you know what is going on.

Back to my original point.

I want you to calculate what an hour of time costs from your ideal customer. Take the average wage of their position and divide it by 2,000. This is their hourly rate. Now multiply that hourly rate by 10.

THIS IS NOW WHAT IT COSTS YOU TO SIT DOWN WITH THEM! By asking for an hour long meeting, you are incurring a debt that you are going to pay off with insight and consulting about your area of expertise.

If your ideal customer makes $1,000,000 per year, you need to offer $5,000 worth of consulting in that hour order to break even with them.

Here is the good news, you know what no one wants to pay for?

Small talk.

As an introvert, you can simply dive right in. You icebreaker can be something as simple as "I know your time is valueable, so I want to make sure we make the most of it."

Now I know what some of you are thinking. What if you offer consulting or coaching services? Why would you give away your product for free?

That is simple.

Stop thinking about consulting as simply offering information. Give away the information and sell the reports and implementation. It is easy to say "Here is what I am thinking" and then charge them to put together a detailed report with step-by-step implementation strategies.

Will some people take the advice and simply never pay you? Probably. But you know as well as I do that the idea is the easy part. The implementation is where things can go wrong without experience.

The biggest thing is to think about how your customer views you and exceed expectations. Offer the kind of consultation that will make them excited to give you referrals. You can do this by behaving in a very un-sales like manner.

All the better for introverts!

12. FEAR ITSELF

Extreme fear can neither fight or fly.

-WILLIAM SHAKESPEARE

I want to talk about policing. Particularly the way police handle protests.

During the Black Lives Matter protests of 2020, I was introduced to a term known as "kettling".

During a protest, police will surround protestors and keep them in one area. They can then compress that area using police with riot shields. This keeps the protestors contained in a small area.

But it also makes them afraid.

Imagine a bunch of police in black riot gear closing in on you. Even if they are not being overtly aggressive, the outfit itself implies aggression.

When people are afraid, adrenaline starts pumping. This leads to a fight/flight/freeze response.

There have been a number of studies done into adrenaline responses, and it turns out that the "fight" option comes up roughly 4% of the time. So, if there are 25 protestors, there is a good chance one of them will respond to fear with aggression. Same thing if there are 25 police officers and they feel afraid.

So if you get 100 protestors and 25 police officers, there are now at least 5 people willing to throw the first punch when things get tense. Then the groups go in to defend each other and you have a full-blown brawl.

What does this have to do with sales?

Well, our brains are not as sophisticated as we like to believe. There are only so many chemicals and hormones that our brains have the ability to utilize. When we feel trapped, our brain will release adrenaline.

It does not matter whether what makes us feel trapped. Are we trapped with a lion? A cop in riot gear? A protestor with a molotov cocktail?

Or a pushy salesperson.

Trapped is trapped. Addrenaline is going to flood your brain either way.

Odds are, however, you probably never had punches thrown during a sales call. So how does fight/flight/freeze manifest during a sales call?

> **Fight:** *Arguing and objections.*
> **Flight:** *I do not want to do this.*

>   *Freeze:* Let me thing about it.

I bet those are very familiar.

Now think about the way most sales scripts are written.

>   *Salesperson:* So do you like water?
>   *Prospect:* Umm, yeah
>   *Salesperson:* Do you like CLEAN water.
>   *Prospect:* Obviously
>   *Salesperson:* (Springing trap) That is great. so here is our water filtration system. It is only $3,995. Do you want us to install it Tuesday or Wednesday?

Now how is that customer going to respond?

>   **Fight:** "Fuck you!"
>   **Flight:** Hang up.
>   **Freeze:** "Umm.... what?"

You see, when one of these three things

happen, it is our fault. We made the customer fearful. We showed up to a conversation with aggressive tactics, made them uncomfortable, and then blamed them for escalating.

"Oh, that guy doesn't *get it*"

Most introverts have felt that discomfort. We are tuned in to what it feels like to be in a high pressure situation. Approach your customers with empathy. Know that trapping them will often make them argue, run away, or be paralyzed by indecision.

Do not create high pressure situations and then pretend to be surprised when someone explodes.

13. THE RABBIT HOLE

The little girl just could not sleep because her thoughts were way too deep, her mind had gone out for a stroll and fallen down the rabbit hole.

-LEWIS CAROLL

Introverts can struggle when it comes to research, but not the way extroverts do. We are good at doing research, but knowing where to stop isn't always our strong suit. As an introvert, I know I want all the possible data that may come up prior to a sales call, but this is way too much to ask. There must be a limit. Otherwise, you cross the line into just avoiding the call. It is a delicate balance between feeling confident and avoidance.

If you want to have high quality conversations, you need to do research. You cannot just walk in blind.

Multi-dialers have become all the rage. A multi-dialer is a tool that does multiple phone calls and once and only connects a salesperson to the like if a real person answers.

If you are selling a simple direct-to-consumer product, a multi-dialer is great. But I know I would rather there be some level of personalization to any call that I get. (We are back to behaving the same way as a marketer as we do as a consumer.) If I take my time to answer a call, I do not want to talk about problems I do not have.

One of my favorite structures for a cold message is **Problem - Implication - Solution**. This is a simple way to explain what you do in one sentence.

*I help (**Ideal Customer**) solve (**Problem**) before it becomes (**Implication**) by (**Solution**).*

For example:

*I help **introverted salespeople** get **better at sales** before they **burnout** by **offering training that focuses on efficiency and emotional intelligence.***

Or:

*I help **small business owners** reduce **employee churn** before it becomes a **major cost issue** through my **book on workplace culture.***

Or:

*I talk to **manufacturing companies** get **sell overseas** without **making the common mistakes most companies make** by offering **international culture training and fit assesment tools.***

If you do not have a statement like this already, take the time to do so. This is also a great profile heading on LinkedIn and is a great way to ask for referrals.

So if we are using this line to start a conversation, we need to be able to make assumptions on where the conversation will go.

These are some good things to know before a call:

-        Job title
-        Recent Social Media Posts
-        Recent articles/podcasts they may have done.
-        Their current vendor/supplier
-        Overall job responsibilities
-        Preferred method of contact. (They may have "call me" or "email me" on certain posts.)

Remember, you are a professional. You need to know your part of the business better than anyone else.

Any and all of these things can help you uncover a problem. You can then tweak your opening li ne based on the problem that you find. **THAT IS THE GOAL OF THE RESEARCH!!!** You want to get enough information to make an assumption about a problem they likely have.

You do not need their life story. You just need to be able to make an educated guess as to a problem they may be experiencing.

Likewise, I suggest avoiding learning anything related to what I call the "small-talk" principles. I teach these using the acronym FORDS.

-        Family / Friends
-        Occupation
-        Recreation
-        Dreams
-        School/Sports.

I would also add weather and traffic. I have seen a number of sales books try to use these as icebreakers. Personally, my favorite icebreaker is "do you mind if we avoid the small talk and get right into what I think I can help you with?"

As an introvert, this should be much easier. You do not need to tip-toe around and make forced small talk about where they went to college or their favorite sports team. You can get right to the point. You use the absolute minimum amount of social battery.

Likewise, **do not limit your research to only the person you are looking to speak to**. One of my favorite things to do is reach out to salespeople in your target organization.

But they are not decision makers and I should only be talking to people who can make the decision. BULLSHIT! Another salesperson is likely going to be the most sympathetic ear you can find. Also, since so many companies hire extroverts, they are probably plugged into all the office gossip.

So many salespeople complain about gatekeepers, but who do you expect to open the gates for you?!?!?! Reach out directly to people within that organization and ask your research questions.

Here is an example of a DM Conversation you can have with another salesperson BEFORE you reach out to your ideal client.

> **YOU**: "Hey, I am wondering if I can ask a little favor salesperson to salesperson."

> **Other Salesperson (OT)** : "What do you need?

> **YOU**: I wanted to get ahold of John Doe, but I have no clue if he is actually who I need to speak to. Can you just tell me if he handles buying widgets for you guys?

> **OT**: You got the wrong person. Jerry FakeName handles that, but we go through ABC Company.

YOU: You are a lifesaver! You probably saved me two weeks of pointless voicemails! Plus you already knew my next question.

OT: Haha! We have all been there.

YOU: Can you tell me, other than price, what is Jerry's biggest headache he wants to avoid?

OT: He HATES Drama. He almost doesn't care about cost so long as you don't give him a headache.

YOU: I get that. And how would you get ahold of him?

OT: He is ALWAYS on his phone! Try texting him.

YOU: Awesome! Do you mind if I drop your name? Either way, I'll fire off some coffee $$$$ if it I get the deal!

Look at that again. Look at what you would have gotten from a conversation like that.

- Best person to contact (Jerry FakeName)
- Their current supplier/vendor (ABC Corp)
- Hot button issues (Drama)
- Best way to contact Jerry. (Text or LinkedIn)

Will you get answers like this all the time? HELL NO! But think about how valuable this is!!! But this conversation will be a lot easier to get than one with someone in the C-Suite.

Now you can research what they currently use (if you haven"t already.) DO NOT JUST GO TO THEIR WEBSITE!!!! It is going to be filled with marketing speak. Instead look at their reviews. Become an expert in your competitors reviews, both good and bad.

Now you can reach out to Jerry. No need for a phone call. You already know he would rather get a Text or a LinkedIn DM.

Remember, this is a "sale" too, even if no money changes hands. You are looking for the currency of your prospect's time and attention. These are some of the most valuable commodities to busy professionals. Offer something in return.

A message like this should work well.

> *"Hey Jerry! Do not worry, I will get right to the point. I already know you use ABC Corp and I am sure you love that they do (Review Research) really well. I also know they can struggle with (Review Research) and it may be creating a headache internally. If I could prove we can make your team more cohesive (Less Drama) do you think I can grab some time on your calendar later this week?"*

How much better is the conversation going to be from here? And guess what, you did not have to make a single phone call yet! That should make your inner introvert happy!

14. LET'S TALK

All salespeople sell the same thing. Change.

-MARCUS CAUCHI

OK, so now you have the appointment, so how do you increase the likelihood that they buy.

Sadly, there is no simple script I can give you. And even if I did have one, I wouldn't suggest you use it. You should be tailoring your approach to each customer's needs, fears, and goals. But I can give you the template for the best sales meetings that will make you look like an expert every single time.

Expectations > Hindsight > Insight > Foresight

I want you to think of **A Christmas Carol** if you have read/seen it before. Each of Dickens' ghosts is a step in the meeting process.

The first ghost does little more than set expectations. "You will be visited by three ghosts".

The second ghost is the ghost of Christmas Past. This is about hindsight. Simply put, what they have been doing and what got them to where they are.

The Third is the ghost of Christmas Present. This is about insight. This is where the ghost showed Scrooge an outside perspective. In A Christmas Carol, it was Bob Cratchitt's family. For you, you are going to open the doors to similar customers in the market and show them what they are doing.

And the last ghost is the ghost of Christmas Yet-To-Come. This is Foresight. This is where you show what would happen if they do and do not make any changes.

Let's go through these one at a time.

1)   *Set Expectations:*

Generally speaking, people are not upset with bad news. They are upset by surprise bad news. There is a major difference between being fired out of the blue and being fired in a round of layoffs that was announced a month earlier. Yes, both suck, but it is the lack of foresight that is the worst.

Use this to your advantage. When possible, send over a simple agenda for a meeting you are having with a potential buyer. Give them a simple outline of your sales process up front so they are not surprised. You can even use the model I set above as a template.

Meeting agenda for Day / Month Time with
_____

2:00 pm: Start Time - Hindsight

- Take time to understand what you have been doing regarding _____

2:10 pm - Insight

- Talk about companies like yours and their experiences doing things they way you have.

2:20 pm – Foresight

- Talk about where you may be already running into problems and where you may run into problems in the future.
- How we can help prevent those issues. (If applicable)

2:30 pm - Conclusion

- Assuming everything looks good, we will ask that _____ (sign contract, make payment, set up meeting, etc)

Do you see how easy that is? You can go much more detailed and lay out some of the questions ahead of time. This way the prospect knows what will come up.

Likewise, you will want to revisit the agenda before you start your meeting. Be open about what you are going to ask for at the end of the meeting.

Do not be coy about pricing. Don't hide it from them. It is OK to give them a range if you do not know for sure. "We have options that range from $___ to $___. I do not want to sell you more than you need because you can always get more later. However, I do not want to sell you something that does not solve the issues you have either."

This can be difficult if you do consulting, however. Sometimes they just need a few sessions, sometimes I have to create a complex curriculum for a long sales cycle alongside a recruiting strategy. At that point my price can be anywhere from a couple thousand dollars to hundreds of thousands of dollars. There is no point in me giving a range that broad.

I cannot give a price without knowing the

problem. So I set up expectations that in the end, I will talk about what I am seeing as issue and put together a loose strategy along with cost. I let them pick the price they want to pay, *but not until they understand the problems they have.* I then create a solution based on doing the most repair I can provide given their budget.

Whatever and however your company does things, be clear about what will happen at the end of the call. Surprising them will lead to an adrenaline response. This will lead to

2)   *Hindsight*

Since you are not an omnipotent ghost, you are going to have to ask questions. This is where your skills as an introvert really come in. Introverts tend to be very inquisitive and conscientious. We like details and enjoy jumping down complex rabbit holes. This is your time to shine a magnifying glass on one part of their life/business that may be a little neglected.

Here are some examples of good questions when you are in the hindsight part of the process.

For those of you familiar with SPIN Selling by Neil Rackham, Focus on the Problem and Implication questions here.

- So I know you are using _____ and like it, but have you ever seen ___?
- How much of your team is actually using ___? What would happen if we get that to 100%?
- I know one of the biggest issues _____ like you face is _____, how have you been dealing with it?

This is where you formulate your plan moving forward, it is also where massive pitch decks and Powerpoints let introvertssalespeople down. Stop assuming you know all of your clients problems and ask. No reason to drag them through 6 slides about a problem they are not facing.

Mini Note: This part of the conversation is commonly called "Discovery", but the word didn't fit with my motif.

3)   Insight

This is where you being an introvert should really pay off, and it is where you get to showcase your expertise. You now get to expand the viewpoint beyond your prospect's walls. You get to take them on a metaphorical guided tour of what their competitors are doing. Who wouldn't love that?

The big thing to accomplish in this part of the talk is getting everyone on the same side! It is not You Company vs. Their Company. It is both companies against the problems you all uncovered together. The insight you are really trying to offer is clarity on the real problem.

Think of it like the last time you got the

sick. Did you complain that you got the flu? Or did you complain that you were cold, nauseous, had a runny nose and a massive headache? Most people are the same. They will complain about the symptoms, and not identify the virus.

A lot of companies come to me and complain that their sales team lacks confidence. But if the whole team lacks confidence, there has to be a common denominator.

This is when I ask Problem focused question like

- How do you decide your company quota?
- How often do you do training?
- What kind of turnover are you experiencing?
- How do you guys celebrate deals?
- What do you do when a salesperson underperforms?

These are simply uncovering the issues.

From here I can uncover the bigger implications behind their answers. If more than 50% of their team is missing quota, how does that impact morale?

I recently got off a call with someone looking for sales training. They were doing weekly training, which is great, but it was all product focused. It was about the niche things that their software can do.

This is all great, but it is what a customer service team is for. Customer service is supposed to understand the product, *sales is supposed to understand the customer*.

Once I understood the training process, I was able to ask questions about turnover. I knew that bad training usually leads to turnover. It turns out they were actually having turnover issues. A salesperson even put their two weeks in THAT MORNING! While the employee said all the right things like he loved working there and he was just offered a better opportunity, we can assume it did not just fall out of the sky.

While we may never know why that salesperson left because he does not want to burn bridges, there may have been others that said the very thing I am talking about outloud.

It is entirely plausible, and even likely that the problem we are discussing was the root cause of the salesperson leaving. The lack of sales training can lead to a stagnation which can lead to a lack of motivation which can lead to a lack of confidence.

Now, we are not just talking about plateauing revenue. We are talking about great employees falling through the gaps. We are talking about hundreds of hours of training that disappeared. And worse, if nothing is done, it can happen again!

Can you see how powerful this is?

Now we uncovered not only the real issue, but the recurring cost of not fixing that

issue.

That needs to be your goal during the consultation.

The insight you provide is the correct diagnosis of the illness, not the symptoms, and the ramifications if the illness is not cured.

You do this by understanding the overall market and what they are doing. You cannot get a good insight without really gathering hindsight.

4)   *Foresight*

Now that you have your diagnosis, you can lay out the future. You can be the Ghost of Business Yet-To-Come.

If you asked the right problem and implication questions, you should have a pretty good idea of the illness and what would happen if it goes untreated.

What happens if someone with the flu goes untreated for a long period of time? It can turn into pneumonia, permanently damage the lungs and in extreme cases lead to death.

What happens if someone with the flu takes medicine? Well they will still feel gross for another few days and then be fine.

Now the key here is that you need to paint an honest picture. If you diagnosed that they do not have a flu, but only a simple cold, then tell them that. They do not need medicine. They need some hot tea, some orange juice, and a couple days in bed. Misdiagnosis leads to malpractice!!!

Through this framework of **Expectation > Hindsight > Insight > Foresight** you give them the wider perspective they need.

You can lay out all the paths in front of them. There should be at least two. **What happens if they do nothing** and **What happens if they get your product/service?**

You should have gotten a pretty good picture of this during the INSIGHT phase, but now you lay out all of your findings.

You job is to help your customers see a wide perspective. They are ground level firefighters simply trying to put out the fire that is in front of them. Your job is to be the person in the helicopter giving them real-time information.

5)   Closing

Let me say this, I hate the emphasis on closing in the sales industry. It is trash!!!

Closing comes at the end of the sales every time. You should not be pushing to close on every single buying signal. This will only piss people off and burn you out faster! Let's keep your closing statement simple.

Is this something you want to move forward with?

This is the only close you need for almost any industry. No need for all the alternative close, assumptive close, standing-room-only close, my-pen-or-yours close, Columbo close bullshit.

If you did steps A-to-Y correctly, step Z should be a foregone conclusion. You should not need to trick and manipulate them into anything. You can just ask for the deal. Be direct.

Likewise, if they say no, then it is either not a fit OR you missed a step and did not address a key concern.

Notice too that I said "move forward". Not buy. There can be many different stages of a sale. Sometimes you are asking for cash. Other times you are asking for more time, a copy of their invoices, a meeting with another person, contact the legal team, etc.

This is why you set expectations. They should know what you are going to ask for in the end. This takes all the pressure off asking for it.

15. OBJECTION!

Don't raise your voice. Improve your argument.

-DESMOND TUTU

There was a time there was a holy trinity of sales. It was closing techniques, objective handling, and open-ended questions. I think all three are a bit of a waste, but if you want more detail why I would suggest reading SPIN Selling by Neil Rackham. He rips these things apart better than anyone else.

To keep it short, let me put it this way. The best sales happen with the fewest objections.

I want you to think of your most problematic customer. What was their sales process like?

Now think of your favorite customer? What was their process like?

My guess was one of them was contentious and argumentative from the start. They kept demanding more and more and more until you begin begging your managers to fire them.

The worst clients require the most objection handling and closing techniques. Virtually every customer I had to fight to "close" became a headache later on. It was not a fit to begin with, and by forcing it I was only creating bigger issues.

Before you know it I am spending a ton of time managing a tiny account I do not even really want to work with anyway.

We are going to do something different. We are not going to spend a ton of time talking about objection handling techniques. I am going to tell you something I wish someone told me earlier in my career.

Ready?

The best way to handle objections is to not get them at all!!!

I know. It sounds much easier said than done. But let's assume it is possible for a moment. How would you do it?

First, as I said earlier, people are not as upset by bad news as they are upset by *surprise* bad news. So don't avoid the bad news. Tell people right up front. Be open and honest the whole time.

Imagine saying "here is what you won't like about my product, but here is why you should get it anyway." How much trust does that build right away? I am not hiding anything from you. I will even give you the ammunition to say no to me.

People are conditioned not to trust salespeople when they tell them something. They believe most salespeople are only out for their own interests and will hide information if it serves our purpose. PROVE THEM WRONG.

When I sell coaching and training, I say this kind of thing all the time.

"If you are looking for me to give you a magic set of words that will make you a multi-millionaire. In fact you will probably fight against some of the suggestions I make. I am not here to make this comfortable for you. The comfortable thing would be to make no change and stay where you are."

The idea is to position things where it is not you and the customer fighting. It is you and the customer against the problem, not you against the customer.

Second, if you want fewer objections, ask more questions. Customer may suggest you tweak the phrasing, but they cannot scream bullshit at a question. They can scream bullshit during a monologue.

The more questions you ask, the fewer objections you will come across. You will also be able to understand what their problems are BEFORE they come up.

Do you know who gets the most objections? The people with a 23-page Powerpoint presentation that dives into the Features, Advantage, and Benefits of every nut and bolt.

Don't be that person.

Set yourself up as an alliance against the problems in their life and they will not object to much of anything!

16. RECHARGE

It is time for people in business to take steps to recharge the workplace.

-CHUCK MARTIN

So most of this book so far has been mostly how-to-sell advice. It has been really focused on the technical side of sales. When doing my research for this book, one of the major complaints I saw was the books were just sales books that loosely tied in introversion, or there was not enough concrete strategy. I must admit, I am trying to thread the needle here.

Everything I have really offered up to this point has meant to be very practical advise you can put into practice (if you haven't already). But now we need to talk about the softer side of sales some more.

You see, a recent study of 700 salespeople found that 63% were dealing with mental health issues (Anxiety, depression, etc). It is not only the elephant in the room. It is the elephant sitting on our chest and making it hard for us to breath.

Introverts, by our very nature, are very inwardly focused. It is literally where the word comes from. And when something is wrong with our mental health, everything suffers.

This is not an issue with "hustle", "Fake it till you make it", or "get out of your comfort zone". This is about creating a model that does not lead to burnout. This is about building something sustainable for the long term.

Remember the Intro I explained the idea of stimulus. We need to dive back into that.

I want you to remember the last time you were bored at home for whatever reason. You start feeling antsy and need to get out of the house. At this point, you call a friend and go and have a coffee with them.

Now you are comfortable.

But there is a problem. Now your friend is bored. They want to go and do something active! They don't want to just sit in a coffee shop. So they drag you to their gym to do a Zumba workout.

It is loud, sweaty, and there are way too many people. You hate it!!!

This was a simple journey that took you from under stimulated to comfortable and then to over stimulated.

Now let's add another step to the journey. Your friend sees someone at the Zumba Class who says that the two of you NEED to go to this new nightclub. She will not take no for an answer. The three of you go to the nightclub.

Now, what happened is really interesting, because now your friend, who was bored at the coffee shop and comfortable at the Zumba class, is now suffering over-stimulation. And you are likely WAY overstimulated!

It like shower temperature. What is just-right for some can be too cold or too hot for others.

Your job, as an introvert, is to keep yourself at the right temperature as often as you can.

Why do I use this analogy? It is simple.

Do you remember being in an office that is either way to cold or way too hot? Do you think you did your best work that day?

Of course not!

You were so pre-occupied on being uncomfortable that you couldn't get anything done.

Stimulus is the same way. Too much or too little and it is all you can think about. It is why some people like having headphones on when they work and other people (like myself) need quiet. Other people like doing their work in a Starbucks because of the level of ambient activity. It is about putting yourself in the right environment to do your best and most efficient work.

When we were talking about sales goals, we laid out something simple. Our goal was to **double** how effective we are at booking appointments. We wanted to go from making 1,000 calls to 500 calls while making the same number of appointments.

Discomfort will keep us from our goals!

Customers are much more emotionally in

tuned than we give them credit for. They can pick up any level of discomfort we have. When they do, customers do not usually think "well maybe the room is just hot" or "maybe there is a song on they do not like." They think we are lying.

Think about watching a hostage video where they are holding a newspaper claiming they are not being mistreated. The hostage looks clean and healthy with no bumps or bruises, but you see their hands shaking and hear a tremor in their voice. What assumption are you going to make?

Now, imagine that same hostage is actually being treated really well. He has a King sized bed, video games systems, great food, and is even invited to poker night with some of the hostage takers. But yet despite all of this, he is still nervous and shaking during the video. What would explain his behavior?

What is he is just camera shy? There is no abuse, in fact the hostage is having the time of his life! But everyone who watches the video will assume the hostages are hiding something.

I am not saying salespeople are looked at as hostage takers, but there is a reason for the prejudice against us. And since that bias is there, we need to do all we can to make sure that distrusting voice doesn't start speaking in our customer's minds.

If we do not take the time to recharge our batteries, our customers will see our discomfort. They will hear it in our voices and see it in the way our shoulders sag. And they will jump to the most obvious conclusion; we are lying.

This is why building an environment where we stay as charged as possible is important. Finding the right environment where we can stay plugged-in as long as possible is the best way to avoid customers thinking something is wrong.

Running on empty will keep us from our

goals!

Ideally, we would find a way to sell that recharges us. We would create a process where we are constantly charging. This is unlikely. Being happy all the time is unrealistic. But how close can we get? If we could get just a little bit closer to that, it can have a serious impact on how well we do.

17. HABITAT

A truly healthy environment is not only safe but stimulating.

WILLIAM H. STEWART

The last thing you need to think of as an introverted salesperson is your habitat. I say last because it is likely the one you have the least say over right now. If you are a small business owner you may have some leeway, but as a rank-and-file salesperson you may not have much choice in enclosing your work space in soundproofing materials and keeping the door closed.

Controlling your environment and your mindset does create tangible results though. While these things do not seem like a big deal, they can drain your battery and make you less effective when you finally do get in front of customers.

Here are a few things I recommend introverts avoid when possible.

Open Concept Offices: These have become all the rage. They are also enraging! I do not want to hear when every phone rings or be able to see everyone on their lunch break while I am trying to find the exact word for the right email. These may seem like they are not a big deal, but having worked in an open concept office I will suggest avoiding them.

I know it takes me 15-20 minutes to get to a point where I can accomplish deep-thought related work. Every interruption resets that clock to zero and I have to start over. It may not sound like much, but being within an earshot of a conversation about Fantasy Football can totally mess up my rhythm. Before you know it I have re-written the same email 3 or 4 times because a good song come on the radio!

This is not the case for everyone. Remember, it is about stimulus temperature. But I know introverts in particular can struggle in their environment.

Micromangement: I know this is something everyone hates, but it is really bad for introverts. For one, we tend to internalize interactions more than our extroverted counterparts. Micromanagement makes us feel like we are not trusted and kills our confidence.

As a disclaimer, micromanagement is often misdiagnosed. Sometime micromanagement is just the management of people who do not want to work. I am not talking about that.

Micromangement is when an outsized emphasis is placed on something that does not drive results. It is about creating and enforcing complex solutions to minor problems.

My mind thinks back to the movie *Casino* where Robert DeNiro's character wanted the baker to hand count the exact same number of blueberries in each muffin. Sure, having product inconsistencies is problematic, but simply keeping the miser on another minute would solve the same problem.

Micromanagment is toxic for everyone, but it is really bad for introverts. Since we spend so much time evaluating and over-evaluating, that micromanagment is often interpreted as a lack of trust.

Once we perceive a lack of trust, it is a short step to over-analyzing our weaknesses. From there it is an even shorter step to get to a lack of confidence and plummeting sales results.

Avoid this whenever you can when choosing a workplace. Micromanagement is bad for everyone, but worse for introverts.

Multitasking: Multitasking is simply an additional battery drain. Like I stated before, it takes me 15 minutes or so to get my head in the zone. I even accommodate for this in my scheduling. And odds are the tasks require different parts of your brain.

You have likely heard that "we only use 10% of our brain". Well it is not really true. It is more accurate to say we can only use 10% of our brain at a time.

For instance, when I am writing this book, I need to use my Parietal Lobe. That is the part of the brain that governs language. But I also have a 2-year old daughter, and watching her requires me to be emotionally available. That is focused on the neocortex. Trying to run both systems at the same time is like trying to drive 2 cars with the same battery. There just isn't enough "power" to run both.

As introverts, our battery is the most important thing to protect, and running too many systems off it at once is a big predictor of burnout.

If you are reading a job description that asks for multi-taskers, run away!

Music: Yes, we all love music, and there is a good chance that you have music on while you are reading this book. But there can be certain kinds of music that can make things more difficult. Personally, I do not want to listen to anything with lyrics while I am working. It is too easy for me to get pulled off track. Next thing I know I end up emailing a client the Wu Tang lyrics by mistake.

Get the money.

Dolla Dolla Bills, ya'll.

Be sure to also keep in mind the rabbit-hole effect regarding music. Introverts are great at being curious and searching for complex answers. But this cuts both ways. Have you ever heard a song and then tried to remember what movie it was from? When music is playing all the time, it is easy for a simple classic-rock ear worm to burrow into your subconscious and eat a massive chunk of your day!

Personally, there is one song I know that is all instrumental. There are no lyrics, but I know it as the song from *GoodFellas* when they find Carbone in the freezer. Every time I here it my mind mentally watch that scene, and most of *Goodfellas* by memory. If you only have so much battery each day, do not waste it watching movies in your own head or having Hakuna Matata on repeat in your head.

Content Creation: One last thing to consider is a content creation space. I am a big fan of leveraging podcasts and videos to grow your sales career, and I am sure you noticed.

Given that I wrote an entire chapter on using content marketing to show off your expertise, you want to have an environment where you can create content when you need to. But this is not something you can do anywhere.

Places with a lot of hard surfaces, like tile, metal, and glass can do horrible things to sound quality. Likewise you do not want to do videos with nothing more than a plain white wall behind you.

Try to pick a place that you can create content whenever possible. The goal is to be able to create content once and use it for years. So keep this in mind when looking for a place to work.

From a video perspective, think about what is behind you. Is it interesting enough to make someone watch but not so busy that viewers will spend the whole time seeing what is on your shelves? You so not want a window behind you because you will likely be totally backlit. And lastly you do not want a ton of people walking right behind you or people starting conversations with cubicle neighbors while you are recording.

From an audio perspective, think soft surfaces and good microphone. There are a ton of sound dampening products on

Amazon, so start there. Some of them even look good enough to have behind you on videos.

Side note, one of the best places you can shoot videos is in your car. There is a ton of sound dampening material along with nearly 360 degrees of natural light.

18. DON'T D.I.Y.

If it doesn't say Binford on it, someone else probably made it.

-TIM "THE TOOL MAN" TAYLOR

Ok, so the ultimate goal is to have something that creates maximum results from minimal social battery. This means we need to know where to focus our efforts so minimal energy creates maximum results. We cannot be everywhere at once, and our most valuable resource we have is that social battery. All of our sales will have to use some of that charge, so wasting time with activities that drain the battery and do not create the results we are looking for.

I say this because you should not do everything related to sales alone! It is not worth it. Leverage other people and tools to grow your sales. Here are some of my favorite tools for you to know. You likely know most, if not all of them, but you may not be using them the same way. (FYI: I am not getting paid by any of these companies right now, but would if they offered!)

- LinkedIn
- YouTube
- Video messenger like Vidyard or BombBomb
- Facebook
- Reddit
- Prospect Safari
- Canva.com
- Copy.ai
- Amazon
- Fiver / Upwork

LinkedIn: This one should be obvious for any of us in the BTB space. But I am talking about using it for networking. I have grown my

LinkedIn profile considerably, and now I can leverage a community for all sorts of things. Yes, I can use it for creating posts and finding customers. I also used it for the research to write this book. I also would have used it in the example I gave where you reach out to another salesperson.

YouTube: You do not need to have a big following to use YouTube for sales. I mentioned doing simple videos of the Frequently Asked Questions and sending them in emails to cold prospects. This is something you can do right now and re-use the videos for years!

Video Messenger: I refuse to leave voicemails anymore. The response rate is trash. Instead I will either send a text or send a video email. I can say the exact same thing I would have in the voicemail, but it is so much more effective and has a higher response rate. I would also say I love video for long emails. I do not want to spend a half hour writing up and editing an email. I would rather record what I need to in a few minutes and fire it off. And while saving time alone is worth it, it also cuts down on miscommunication because the tone seemed off.

Facebook: I do not like Facebook. I do not care that my aunt had her first baloney sandwich in years. But I do love Facebook Groups. I have set up countless podcast interviews through Facebook that have turned into business. I have also been able to join groups and see what my ideal customer are talking about in order to improve the messages that I send.

Reddit: Reddit is the least likely sales tool on this list, but it is great for research. The level of open and honest conversations along with advice on Reddit is amazing. Do not underestimate it!

Prospect Safari: I will start by saying I am a little biased here as the CEO is a friend. But Prospect Safari ties into most major CRMs and can help you find prospects that are not on LinkedIn, Seamless or ZoomInfo. As of this writing you can get 50 leads for free so give them a shot.

Canva: An platform to create images. I have used it for just about any graphic design I need. The free version has its limits, but still does what I need it to.

Copy.ai: This one is not perfect, but I still like it when I am scratching my head about what to send. You can plug in a few keywords and the tool will use artificial intelligence to create some sales copy for you. No, it is not perfect, but it is one of my favorite tools when I am trying to wonder what to post.

Amazon: Another undervalued resource tool. Not from a commerce side, but from a customer research side. Amazon reviews are a great place to find out what really bothers your customers. I look at the reviews for books all the time and copy-and-paste the insightful ones into a file. I can then re-phrase and use these for posts or emails.

Fivver / Upwork: I will be honest that I have used both and had good results on both of them. I use these tools most for the boring work like keyword research or search engine optimization (SEO) that I hate. If I record a video or write a blog I can spend $20 and get someone to help do all the work I hate so I can focus on things like writing this book. These are for tasks that are worth doing but not worth doing myself.

19. CONCLUSION

Show me the way to go home. I'm tired and I want to go to bed. I had a little drink about an hour ago and its gone right to my head.

-DRINKING SONG FROM *JAWS*

Well, I over-did it.

When I started writing this Min-E-Book, I expected it to be about 1,800 words.

Oops.

I kept thinking about my own struggles in the sales world and what I wished people told me earlier. This book ballooned from there.

My sales career started when I was fresh out of college, but I did not hit my stride until I hit rock bottom. I sat in the parking lot of a factory crying and having a panic attack. I was crying and hyperventilating.

There is a joke by Tommy Johnagin has after he went through a bad breakup. Someone asked if he cried like a baby. His response: "I didn't cry like a baby, I cried like a grown man. Babies do not have the lung capacity to make the noises I did."

I say this because my story should be among the worst-case scenarios for introverts in the sales world. I spent years pushing harder and harder. I would go above and beyond KPI targets but not hitting quota. I kept going until I was burnt out and broken down.

I am lucky. I bounced back. I started reading books like this and crawled back up from rock bottom.

That is good news, but here is better news.

You do not have to be like me.

You can make changes now before you hit the point that I did.

That is the beautiful thing about rock bottom. You get to choose it. You can say, at any point, that you will no longer accept the situation you are in. You can decide to make changes.

You do not even have to wait for anything really bad to happen. You can run out of coffee tomorrow morning, decide "I will no longer accept this" and build an empire of Dunkin Donuts franchises.

That is possible. But only if you understand yourself, your strengths, and build a career that lends itself to what you are already amazing at.

Being an introvert can be a superpower.

It can be the difference between thriving in our new modern economy and being replaced by artifical intelligence software.

There is no escaping the fact that modern sales are going to become more complex. The amount of information buyers already have access to means salespeople will have to be better informed than ever before. Salespeople will need to understand how complicated organizations operate and explain it in simple way. The people who thrive in the future will be the ones who can understand and disseminate information better than anyone else.

Extroverts don't stand a chance.

You've got this!

20. DON'T FORGET

Remember when I set expectations earlier in the book where I would ask for a review in the end. Here I am approaching your table with a leather bifold and the bill for your dinner. I hope you enjoyed it!

Please take the time to write a review of this book. Please be he honest, because I am going to use that feedback to write the next book. And probably the book after that. Maybe another after that.

I really hope you enjoyed all that you read, but if you did not I want to know that too!

If you would like to know more about

me and what I do, feel free to visit BrokenSalespeople.com.

You can also email me about creating a sales training program for your team at Red@brokensalespeople.com

ACKNOWLEDGEMENT

I could not have completed this book without the help of so many people.

First, I want to Thank my wife Amy for taking our daughter to her mother's so I could focus and write in quiet. It was one of the most productive times I have ever had.

To Pops for all the help with everything. Not to mention being a sounding board after calls.

To Marcus Cauchi for bringing me into TRT and treating me like a member of the team as the greenest one on the bunch!

To Fraser Hay for giving me the confidence

and expertise I needed to put something like this together

And to Mandy O'Neill for helping me with rebuilding everything and getting me on this track.

There are so many more! Thank you all so much!

ABOUT THE AUTHOR

Red Stafstrom

Red Stafstrom is a sales trainer, author, podcast host, nerd, and father who spends way too much time listening to audiobooks. After graduating college to be a  history teacher, Red fell into a sales role and stayed. He spent years learning the kinds of sales he would not wish on his worst enemies. While it took him much longer than it should have, he eventually started to rebuild everything he every learned about sales.

Red now does training as the founder of Broken Salespeople which focuses on teaching emotionally intelligent sales techniques.

You can find him easiest on LinkedIn, but you can also follow the Broken Salespeople Youtube page. You can also check out BrokenSalespeople.com.